Twenty to Make

Sugar Fairies

Frances McNaughton

Search Press

First published in Great Britain 2010

Search Press Limited
Wellwood, North Farm Road,
Tunbridge Wells, Kent TN2 3DR

Text copyright © Frances McNaughton 2010

Photographs by Debbie Patterson at
Search Press Studios

Photographs and design copyright
© Search Press Ltd 2010

ISBN: 978-1-84448-561-1

Suppliers
If you have difficulty in obtaining any of the
materials and equipment mentioned in this book,
then please visit the Search Press website for
details of suppliers: www.searchpress.com

Printed in Malaysia

This book is dedicated to Mike.

Contents

Introduction

The fairies in this book are made using a number of techniques suitable for beginners to modelling in sugarpaste, with a few more detailed models for those of you who are more advanced. The basic shapes and tools are kept as simple as possible.

I made my fairies in sugarpaste, coloured with strong paste food colours. Ready-coloured sugarpaste, modelling paste, and the other items you will need are available from specialist sugarcraft shops and online sugarcraft and cake decorating suppliers.

For many of the fairies, I used 'candy sticks', available from sweet shops, for the arms, legs and neck supports. I also used chocolate-covered biscuit sticks and liquorice sticks in different flavours. I used soft fudge sweets, which can be softened in your hand and shaped in the same way as sugarpaste, for the Chocolate Fudge Fairy on page 22. For alternative ideas, look in sweet shops and supermarkets for other sweets which could be used.

A stronger type of modelling paste can be made by kneading a small pinch of CMC (cellulose gum), or gum tragacanth in to sugarpaste. This stronger paste is used for some of the wings and for the standing models, and can be used for making candy sticks for the legs and supports.

The amount of sugarpaste and the approximate conversions I have listed for each model are only intended as a guide; models can, of course, be made in different sizes.

White marzipan could be used to make the models, coloured in the same way as the sugarpaste. Chocolate sugarpastes and modelling pastes are a good way of making brown and cream models and parts without having to use food colours.

The techniques in this book can also be used to make long-lasting model fairies with non-edible modelling pastes such as the air-drying modelling pastes available from craft shops.

Basic materials

Clockwise from left in the picture opposite, **various cutters**: an eight-petal flower cutter, a carnation cutter, a calyx (five-point) cutter, a variety of butterfly cutters, a garrett frill cutter (large, fluted round cutter), circle cutters, an oak leaf cutter, a heart cutter, a tiny blossom cutter and a daisy cutter.

Multi-mould This can be used to make a tiny crown, wings, a tiny flower, a tiny faceted star and other small items useful for making fairies.

Small drinking straw This should be cut off at an angle, and is used for making mouths and closed eyes.

Cocktail stick This is used for various shaping and texturing techniques.

Various tools: a textured frilling tool, a dogbone tool and a Dresden tool.

Cutting wheel This is used for cutting shapes from rolled sugarpaste.

Thin palette knife This is available from sugarcraft shops and art shops. It is useful for releasing sugarpaste from the work surface, and for cutting and marking lines.

Dusting brush This is used for applying edible powder food colour, or edible glitter.

Black or brown **food colour felt-tip pen** This is for making edible marks.

Small paintbrush/ water brush This is used for dampening the sugarpaste to join pieces together, or for applying egg white.

Small non-stick rolling pin For rolling out sugarpaste or modelling paste.

Small plain piping tubes These are for cutting tiny circles for eyes etc.

Various edible pearl colours and **edible glitter** (shown, right) These are used to add a sparkle to fairies.

Other items

To stop paste sticking to your hands and tools, rub a small amount of **vegetable cooking oil** in to your hands and the surface, or sprinkle a small amount of icing sugar. If using icing sugar, be careful not to use too much, as this could dry the paste and cause cracking.

Use **plastic sandwich bags** for storing pieces of sugarpaste. Also, if you have problems rolling paste thinly, place the paste inside the plastic sandwich bag and then roll it.

A **sieve**, **sugarcraft gun** or **garlic press** can be used to create very thin or fluffy looking strands of sugarpaste as for the pompoms for the Christmas Fairy.

Materials for joining sugarpaste shapes

Most parts can be stuck together just by dampening them with water. Make sure that the paste is only dampened – don't wet the surface too much, or the pieces will just slide off. Fresh egg white can also be used as a slightly stickier glue. You can also use thick edible glue. This is useful for attaching dried sugar pieces (for instance the wings and heads) and for when a stronger glue is needed. Mix a pinch of modelling paste with a few drops of water by mashing it with a palette knife until it forms a stringy, sticky glue. If you make this glue with the same colour paste as used on the model, it will be easier to hide.

Rainbow Fairy

Materials:

10g (¹⁄₃oz) flesh-coloured
  sugarpaste for the head

10g (¹⁄₃oz) blue sugarpaste for
  the body

10g (¹⁄₃oz) blue modelling paste
  (see page 4) for the wings

10g (¹⁄₃oz) each red, yellow,
  purple and green sugarpaste

Three candy sticks

Tiny amount of black sugarpaste
  for the eyes

Thick edible glue

Tools:

Tiny blossom cutter

Small drinking straw

Thin palette knife

Non-stick rolling pin

Circle cutters: 22mm (⅞in),
  32mm (1¼in), 41mm (1⅝in),
  56mm (2¼in)

Plastic sandwich bag

Water brush

Dresden tool or cocktail stick

Scrunched up paper tissue

Instructions:

1 For the head, take the flesh-coloured sugarpaste and
pinch off a piece. Use this to make two tiny teardrop
shapes for the ears and a tiny pin-head piece for the nose.
Form the rest into a ball and use a finger to roll a slight
indentation across the middle. Make a hole in the neck end using a dry candy stick.
Attach the nose in the centre of the face, and press a mouth shape with the cut
drinking straw under the nose. Dampen the sides of the head in line with the nose.
Stick the ears on and press in place using a Dresden tool or cocktail stick, forming
the ear shape. Make two tiny pin-head size pieces of black sugarpaste for the eyes.
Dampen the face to stick them on, slightly above the nose.

2 For the wings, roll out the blue modelling paste and cut it with the largest circle cutter. Roll out the green, red and yellow pastes, and cut them using a smaller size of circle cutter for each one. Dampen the surface of the blue circle and attach the green one, then dampen and attach the red, then the yellow. Cut the circle into quarters (this makes two pairs of wings) and leave to dry for a few hours or overnight.

3 Make the shoes with two pea-sized pieces of coloured sugarpaste. Shape to form a point. Dampen the ends of two of the candy sticks and attach the shoes.

4 Make an egg shape of the blue sugarpaste for the body with a candy stick for support, slightly sticking out. Push the legs into the body.

5 Make coloured petals for the skirt using pea-sized pieces of sugarpaste, flattened and thinned at the edge by pressing them in a plastic sandwich bag. Attach the petals around the body.

6 Take a slightly larger than pea-sized piece of coloured sugarpaste for each arm. Roll to form a long carrot shape, shorter than the legs. Flatten the thin end, and cut a little thumb to make the hand. Position the arms and attach them to the body.

7 For the hair, make lots of small carrot-shaped pieces of different coloured sugarpaste. Dampen the head and attach the strands of hair with the pointed end towards the face and neck. When the head is covered with enough strands of hair, cut out some tiny blossoms in different colours and stick on to the top of the head.

8 Dampen the end of the candy stick neck and attach the head, looking to one side.

9 Attach the wings with thick edible glue (see page 7). Prop them up with scrunched-up paper tissue until the glue is dry.

Rose Fairy

Materials:

10g (¹/₃oz) flesh-coloured
    sugarpaste for the head

Red sugarpaste, 10g (¹/₃oz) for
    the body and 10g (¹/₃oz) for
    the hands, shoes and hair

10g (¹/₃oz) red modelling paste
    (see page 4) for the wings,
    rose petal skirt and rose hat

Candy stick

Four strawberry liquorice sticks

Tiny amount of black
    sugarpaste for the eyes

Tools:

27mm (1¹/₈in) heart cutter

Small drinking straw

Non-stick rolling pin

Thin palette knife

Plastic sandwich bag

Water brush

Dresden tool or
    cocktail stick

Scrunched up paper tissue

Instructions:

1 For the wings, roll out the
red modelling paste and cut
out two hearts with the heart
cutter. Roll a cocktail stick over
the rounded edges to frill them slightly. Leave to dry for a few hours or overnight.

2 For the legs, cut two strawberry liquorice sticks to 6.5cm (2½in), and cut them to a
point for the feet. For the shoes, shape two pea-sized pieces of red sugarpaste to a
point. Dampen the pointed ends of the legs and attach the shoes.

3 For the arms, cut two strawberry liquorice sticks to 5cm (2in), and cut them to an angle
for the shoulder ends. For the hands, make two pea-sized pieces of red sugarpaste to
form simple hand shapes, cut out a tiny triangle from each to form thumbs. Dampen the
flat ends of the arms and attach the hands.

5 Make the head as on page 8. Dampen the end of the candy stick neck, and attach the head.

6 Roll out white modelling paste thinly, in a plastic sandwich bag if that helps. Dampen around the bottom of the body and the top of the arms, cut out large blossoms and stick them in place. Dampen the fairy head (but not the face) and attach tiny blossoms all over it. Stick a blossom on each foot.

7 Attach the wings as on page 9.

Pretty in Purple

These fairy friends are just frothing over with flowers. The other little blossom fairy has white legs and purple blossoms.

Stardust Fairy

Materials:

10g (¹⁄₃oz) white sugarpaste for the head

Black sugarpaste: 10g (¹⁄₃oz) for the body, 5g (¹⁄₆oz) for the hat and a tiny amount for the eyes

10g (¹⁄₃oz) white modelling paste (see page 4) for the star wings, skirt and head-dress

Candy stick

Four liquorice sticks

Edible glitter

Thick edible glue

Tools:

Star cutters: large, medium, small and tiny

Small drinking straw

Non-stick rolling pin

Thin palette knife

Plastic sandwich bag

Water brush

Dresden tool or cocktail stick

Scrunched up paper tissue

Instructions:

1 For the wings and head-dress, roll out the white modelling paste and cut three stars with the medium star cutter. Dampen the surfaces of the stars and sprinkle them with edible glitter. Leave to dry for a few hours or overnight.

2 For the legs, cut two liquorice sticks to 6.5cm (2½in), and cut them to a point for the feet. For the shoes, make two pea-sized pieces of white sugarpaste and shape each one to a point. Dampen the pointed ends of the legs and attach the shoes.

3 Roll out white sugarpaste and cut out a large star for the skirt.

4 Make an egg shape of the black sugarpaste for the body with a candy stick for support, slightly sticking out. Attach the star skirt to the bottom of the body. Dampen the underside of the skirt and position the body on top of the legs.

5 For the arms, cut two liquorice sticks to 5cm (2in), and cut each one to an angle for the shoulder end. For the hands, make two pea-sized pieces of white sugarpaste to form simple hand shapes, and cut out tiny triangles to form thumbs. Dampen the flat ends of the arms and attach the hands. Dampen the top ends of the arms and push into the body.

14

6 Make the head as on page 8.

7 For the hat, roll out black sugarpaste and cut out a large star. Dampen and stick to the head with the points towards the face.

8 Roll out white sugarpaste thinly. Cut out small stars and attach to the chest and knees. Cut out tiny stars and attach to the head and shoes.

9 Attach the wings and star head-dress with thick edible glue (see page 7).

You can buy edible glitter in all kinds of different shades to give the stars a colourful shimmer.

Daisy Fairy

Materials:

20g (²⁄₃oz) green modelling paste (see page 4)

5g (¹⁄₆oz) flesh-coloured sugarpaste

5g (¹⁄₆oz) yellow modelling paste

5g (¹⁄₆oz) yellow sugarpaste

10g (¹⁄₃oz) white modelling paste for the wings and daisy petals

Five candy sticks

Tiny amount of black sugarpaste for the eyes

Edible powder food colour, green

Thick edible glue

Tools:

Large butterfly cutter

Dusting brush

Daisy flower cutter

Non-stick rolling pin

Small drinking straw

Thin palette knife

Plastic sandwich bag

Water brush

Dresden tool or cocktail stick

Scrunched up paper tissue

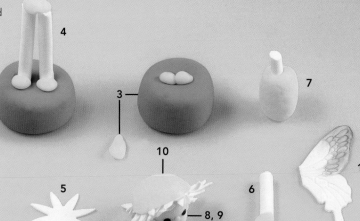

Instructions:

1 Roll out the white modelling paste and cut out a pair of butterfly wings with a large butterfly cutter. Gently brush green powder food colour over the surface. Leave to dry for a few hours or overnight.

2 For the base, shape the green modelling paste to a drum shape.

3 For the shoes, make two small pea-sized pieces of yellow sugarpaste and shape each to an oval. Attach to the top of the drum.

4 For the legs, push two candy sticks straight down through one end of the shoes to the very bottom of the base. This will help support the standing figure. Attach a pea-sized piece of yellow sugarpaste on top of the legs to form the base of the body.

5 Roll out white modelling paste thinly. Cut out two daisy flowers, dampen the centres and stick them one on top of the other on the base of the body to make the skirt.

6 For the arms, cut or break two candy sticks to slightly shorter than the legs. For the hands, make two pea-sized pieces of yellow sugarpaste to form simple hand shapes and cut out a tiny triangle from each to form thumbs. Dampen the ends of the arms and attach the hands.

7 Make an egg shape of yellow modelling paste for the body with a candy stick for support, slightly sticking out for the neck. Dampen the top ends of the arms and push them into the body. Cut out two more daisy flowers and stick them on to form a collar. Attach the body to the top of the legs. Leave to dry overnight, propped upright.

8 Make the head as on page 9.

9 Cut out four more daisy flowers. Cut each flower into segments and stick to the head around the face. Petals can be dried close to the head (main picture, right) or opening out (detail picture, left).

10 Form a ball of yellow sugarpaste, just bigger than a pea. Flatten around the edge, widening it enough to cover the back of the head. Attach it. Texture the surface with a cocktail stick.

11 Attach the wings as on page 9.

12 Use thick edible glue to stick the head on top of the neck.

Vibrant greens and yellows give this flower fairy a wonderfully summery feel. You could make a Michaelmas Daisy fairy with purple petals.

Dancing Fairy

Materials:

10g (⅓oz) flesh-coloured sugarpaste

Pink sugarpaste:
  10g (⅓oz) for the body,
  10g (⅓oz) for the skirt, hands, feet and hair

10g (⅓oz) white modelling paste (see page 4) for the wings

Five candy sticks

Tiny amount of black sugarpaste for the eyes

Thick edible glue

Tools:

Small butterfly cutter

Carnation cutter

Tiny blossom cutter

Non-stick rolling pin

Small drinking straw

Thin palette knife

Plastic sandwich bag

Water brush

Dresden tool or cocktail stick

Scrunched up paper tissue

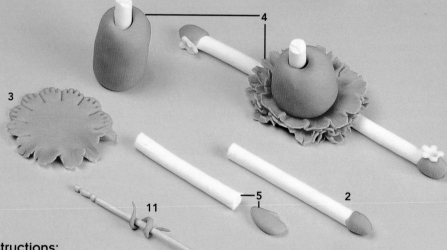

Instructions:

1 Roll out the white modelling paste and cut it with a small butterfly cutter. Leave to dry for a few hours or overnight.

2 Make the legs from two candy sticks. For the shoes, make two pea-sized pieces of pink sugarpaste and shape each to a point. Dampen the ends of the legs and attach the shoes. Make a pea-sized piece of sugarpaste to stick the top ends of the legs together, end to end.

3 For the tutu, roll out thin sugarpaste. Cut out at least three carnation flowers. Frill the edges with a cocktail stick, using icing sugar or cornflour to stop it sticking. Dampen the middle of each and stick one on top of the other on the top of the legs.

4 Make an egg shape of pink sugarpaste for the body with a candy stick for support, slightly sticking out. Dampen the bottom of the body and stick on top of the tutu.

5 For the arms, cut or break two candy sticks to make them slightly shorter than the legs. For the hands, make two pea-sized pieces of pink sugarpaste to form simple hand shapes, then cut out a tiny triangle from each to form thumbs. Dampen the ends of the arms and attach the hands. Stick the arms into the body.

6 Make the head as on page 8.

7 For the hair, roll out a piece of pink sugarpaste slightly larger than a pea, to cover the back of the head. Dampen it and stick it in place. Mark it with a knife to look like hair. Attach a small ball of sugarpaste for a bun.

8 Dampen the end of the candy stick neck and attach the head.

9 Attach the wings as on page 9.

10 Cut out two tiny blossoms from white modelling paste and stick them on the shoes.

11 Make very thin strands of pink sugarpaste and twirl them into coils around a cocktail stick. Dampen the front edge of the hair, and stick the twirls of paste around the edge of the face.

Shall We Dance?

This beautiful fairy and her friend in white and yellow would make lovely cake toppers for a birthday girl who loves dancing.

Baby Fairy

Materials:

White sugarpaste; 100g (3½oz) for the cloud and 5g (⅙oz) for the hat

5g (⅙oz) white modelling paste (see page 4) for the wings

5g (⅙oz) flesh-coloured sugarpaste for the head

15g (½oz) pale blue sugarpaste

Candy stick

Tools:

Small butterfly cutter

Non-stick rolling pin

Small drinking straw

Thin palette knife

Plastic sandwich bag

Water brush

Dresden tool or cocktail stick

Scrunched up paper tissue

Instructions:

1 Roll out the white modelling paste and cut it with the small butterfly cutter. Leave to dry for a few hours or overnight.

2 Shape most of the white sugarpaste to a simple cloud shape. Save a little for the hat.

3 Make the head as on page 8, but make closed eyes by pressing in the drinking straw, making a curve for each eye.

4 Divide the blue sugarpaste into three equal parts. Use one to make an egg shape for the body with a candy stick for support, slightly sticking out. Lay the body on the cloud, allowing space for the head to be added.

5 Make the second part into a sausage shape approximately twice the length of the head, and slightly thinner at each end for the hands. Flatten the hands slightly. Curve the arms forward and attach to the top of the body.

6 Divide the third piece of blue paste in two to make the legs. Roll each one to a carrot shape about twice the length of the body. Bend in half to form a knee. Gently pinch to form the foot. Stick the legs in place.

7 Roll the remaining white sugarpaste to a long carrot shape for the hat. Wind it around the head, starting with the fat end nearest the face, dampening if necessary, and pressing into place. Finish with a point on the back of the head.

8 Attach the wings as on page 9.

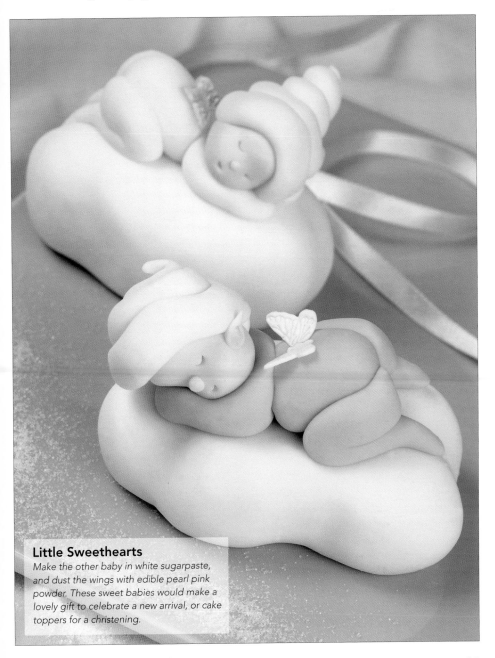

Little Sweethearts
Make the other baby in white sugarpaste, and dust the wings with edible pearl pink powder. These sweet babies would make a lovely gift to celebrate a new arrival, or cake toppers for a christening.

Chocolate Fudge Fairy

Materials:

Commercial soft fudge or
coloured sugarpaste:
10g (¹⁄₃oz) for the head,
10g (¹⁄₃oz) for the body and
10g (¹⁄₃oz) for the shoes,
hands and flowers

10g (¹⁄₃oz) chocolate modelling
paste or brown modelling
paste (see page 4)

Candy stick

Three chocolate biscuit sticks

Tiny amount of black
sugarpaste for the eyes

Tools:

18mm (¾in) heart cutter

Small blossom cutter

Non-stick rolling pin

Small drinking straw

Thin palette knife

Plastic sandwich bag

Water brush

Dresden tool or
cocktail stick

Scrunched up paper
tissue

Instructions:

1 Roll out the brown modelling paste and
cut two wings with a heart cutter. Leave to
dry for a few hours or overnight.

2 The legs are thin chocolate biscuit sticks. For the shoes,
take two pea-sized pieces of fudge and shape each to a point.
Attach the shoes.

3 Make an egg shape of softened fudge for the body with piece of chocolate biscuit
stick for support, slightly sticking out. Push the top end of the legs into the body.

4 Roll out softened fudge. Cut out at least seven heart shapes, and press on to the
body for the skirt. The fudge should stick without you having to dampen the surface.

5 Make the head as on page 8, but use softened fudge.

6 Form tiny shapes of chocolate modelling paste and stick on to the head to give
the appearance of hair.

7 Attach the head to the top of the body.

8 Divide the rest of the chocolate paste to make the arms. Make two sausage shapes and bend them in the middle. Attach the arms to the body, and attach simple hands made from softened fudge.

9 Attach the wings as on page 9.

10 Roll out softened fudge. Cut out small blossoms and press them on top of the head.

Chocolate, biscuit and fudge mean this fairy might not be admired for long – she just looks too tasty!

23

Christmas Fairy

Materials:

10g (⅓oz) flesh-coloured sugarpaste for the head

Green sugarpaste:
10g (⅓oz) for the body and 10g (⅓oz) for the arms and feet

Red sugarpaste:
10g (⅓oz) for the skirt and legs and 10g (⅓oz) for the hat

10g (⅓oz) white sugarpaste for the legs, skirt, fluff and hat

10g (⅓oz) modelling paste (see page 4) for the wings

Candy stick

Tiny amount of black sugarpaste for the eyes

Edible pearl white powder colour.

Tools:

Multi-mould for bird wings

56mm (2¼in) circle cutter

Carnation cutter

Sieve, sugarcraft gun or garlic press

Non-stick rolling pin

Small drinking straw

Thin palette knife

Plastic sandwich bag

Dusting brush

Water brush

Dresden tool or cocktail stick

Scrunched up paper tissue

Instructions:

1 For the wings, press the white modelling paste into the bird wing mould. Remove from the mould and brush with edible pearl white powder. Leave to dry for a few hours or overnight.

2 For the legs, make a red sausage, and a white sausage of sugarpaste, each the size and length wanted for legs. Cut each leg into small segments and put these in a plastic bag to keep them soft. Stick red and white segments together alternately and form two stripey legs. Roll very gently to get the segments attached smoothly (only dampen very slightly if the pieces refuse to stick). Stick the tops of the legs together, side by side.

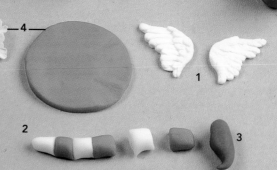

3 For the shoes, make two pea-sized pieces of green sugarpaste and shape each one to a point. Dampen the ends of the legs and attach the shoes.

4 For the skirt, roll out red sugarpaste and cut out a circle using the circle cutter. Frill over the edge with a cocktail stick. Roll out white sugarpaste and cut out a carnation. Frill around the edge as before. Dampen under the two skirt layers and stick them on top of the legs.

5 Make an egg shape of green sugarpaste for the body with a candy stick for support, slightly sticking out. Dampen the bottom of the body and stick it on top of the skirt.

6 Divide the rest of the green sugarpaste and form two carrot shapes for the arms. Bend to form the elbows and flatten the hands. Attach to the body.

7 Make the head as on page 8. Make a cone shape from red sugarpaste for the hat. Hollow the fat end by pressing with your finger and thumb until it fits over the back of the head. Dampen the inside and attach to the head. Bend the point of the hat over to one side.

8 Dampen the end of the candy stick neck and attach the head.

9 Roll a long sausage of white sugarpaste and attach round the edge of the hat.

10 Attach the wings as on page 9.

11 To make pompoms, push a little white sugarpaste through a sieve, sugarcraft gun or garlic press. Dampen the end of the hat and the centre of the chest and attach the pompoms.

This cute fairy is perfect for the Christmas table with her gift of a yellow sweet. If you just want her to be a winter fairy, make her in white sugarpaste, rather than red, white and green.

Daffodil Fairy

Materials:

10g (⅓oz) flesh-coloured
   sugarpaste

10g (⅓oz) orange
   sugarpaste

10g (⅓oz) yellow
   sugarpaste

10g (⅓oz) orange
   modelling paste (see
   page 4) for the wings

Candy stick

Four green liquorice sticks

Tiny amount of black
   sugarpaste for the eye

Tools:

Carnation cutter

Large calyx (five-pointed
   flower) cutter

Tiny six-petal cutter

Small drinking straw

Non-stick rolling pin

Thin palette knife

Plastic sandwich bag

Water brush

Dresden tool or cocktail stick

Scrunched up paper tissue

Instructions:

1 For the legs, cut two green liquorice
sticks to 6.5cm (2½in) and cut them to
points for the feet. For the shoes, make two
pea-sized pieces of orange sugarpaste and shape
each one to a point. Dampen the pointed ends of the legs and attach the shoes.
Attach the tops of the legs to a slightly larger than pea-sized piece of sugarpaste.

2 Roll out yellow sugarpaste and cut out a large calyx for the skirt. Lay the skirt over
the tops of the legs. Cut out two tiny six-petal flowers and stick them on to the shoes.
Make two tiny balls of orange sugarpaste. Stick them on top of the flowers on the
shoes, and make a tiny hole in the middle of each ball.

3 Make an egg shape of the orange sugarpaste for the body with a candy stick
for support, slightly sticking out. Mark a few lines with a knife on the orange paste.
Dampen the bottom of the body and position it on top of the legs.

4 For the arms, cut two green liquorice sticks to 5cm (2in) and cut each one to an angle for the shoulder end. For the hands, make two pea-sized pieces of orange sugarpaste and shape each one into a simple hand, then cut out tiny triangles to form thumbs. Dampen the flat ends of the arms and attach the hands. Dampen the top ends of the arms and push them into the body.

5 Roll out orange modelling paste thinly. Cut out two carnation flowers. Frill around the edge with a cocktail stick. Attach one over the neck for a collar. Cut the second one in half and stick the straight edges along the backs of the arms to make the wings.

This bright and breezy fairy would be perfect for someone with a spring birthday, or for St David's Day.

6 Make the head as on page 8.

7 For the hair, make lots of small carrot-shaped pieces of yellow sugarpaste. Dampen the head and attach the strands of hair with the pointed ends towards the face and neck. When the head is covered with enough strands of hair, dampen the end of the candy stick neck and attach the head.

8 Cut out and frill another orange carnation flower and attach to the back of the head.

Little Princess Fairy

Materials:

White modelling paste (see page 4); 20g (²/₃oz) for the base and 5g (¹/₆oz) for the body

10g (¹/₃oz) modelling paste for the wings, arms, skirt, crown and bow

5g (¹/₆oz) flesh-coloured sugarpaste

5g (¹/₆oz) yellow sugarpaste

Three candy sticks

Tiny amount of black sugarpaste for the eyes

Edible powder food colour pearl white

Edible glitter

Thick edible glue

Tools:

Small butterfly cutter

Multi-mould for the crown

Garrett frill cutter (large fluted round cutter)

Dusting brush

Non-stick rolling pin

Small drinking straw

Thin palette knife

Plastic sandwich bag

Water brush

Dresden tool or cocktail stick

Scrunched up paper tissue

Instructions:

1 For the wings, roll out the white modelling paste and cut out two butterflies with the small cutter. Gently brush pearl white powder food colour over the surface. Leave to dry for a few hours or overnight.

2 For the base, shape the white modelling paste to a drum shape.

3 For the shoes, make two pea-sized pieces of white sugarpaste and shape each to a point. Attach to the top of the drum. For the legs, push two candy sticks straight down through one end of the shoes to the very bottom of the drum. This will help support the standing figure. Attach a pea-sized piece of white sugarpaste on top of the legs to form the base of the body. To decorate the stand I used a length of twirly marshmallow, pushed a candy stick in one end then wrapped the marshmallow around the base. The other end of the candy stick was then pushed into the end of the marshmallow to secure it, at the back of the base.

4 Roll out white modelling paste thinly. Cut out one garrett frill. Frill around the edge with a cocktail stick. Dampen the centre and stick on top of the base of the body to make the skirt. Stick the skirt on top of the legs, making it shorter at the front and longer at the back.

5 Make an egg shape of white modelling paste for the body with a candy stick for support, slightly sticking out for the neck. Dampen it and attach it on top on the legs and skirt. Leave to dry overnight.

6 Cut out a thin strip of rolled-out white modelling paste to make the ribbon waistband. Dust with pearl white powder. Dampen around the waist and attach the ribbon. Join at the back and cut off the excess.

7 For the bow, cut two ribbon tails from sugarpaste, dust with pearl white and attach at the join of the waistband. Cut out a short ribbon, twice the length of the desired bow. Dust, as before. Dampen the middle point of the ribbon and bring both ends into the middle to stick. Stick on to the top of the ribbon tails. Finish with a short piece of dusted ribbon across the middle of the bow.

This sweet fairy is sure to delight the little princess in your life!

8 Divide 5g (¹⁄₆oz) of the sugarpaste and form two carrot shapes for the arms. Bend to form the elbows and flatten the hands. Attach to the body.

9 Attach the wings as on page 9. Attach the other butterfly to the hands.

10 Make the head as on page 8.

11 For the hair, make short carrots of yellow sugarpaste. Attach to the head, shaping into a style and marking strands with a Dresden tool.

12 Make a crown in the mould. Dampen it and sprinkle it with edible glitter. Attach it to the top of the head.

13 Use thick edible glue to stick the head on top of the neck.

Bathing Fairy

Materials:

Flesh-coloured sugarpaste:
  10g (¹⁄₃oz) for the head,
  10g (¹⁄₃oz) for the body and
  10g (¹⁄₃oz) for the arms

10g (¹⁄₃oz) blue sugarpaste

10g (¹⁄₃oz) modelling paste
  (see page 4) for the wings

Candy stick

Tiny amount of black
  sugarpaste for the eyes

Edible blue powder colour

Pretty teacup filled with
  sugarpaste

Extra white sugarpaste
  for bubbles

Tools:

Large butterfly cutter

56mm (2¼in) circle cutter

Non-stick rolling pin

Small drinking straw

Thin palette knife

Plastic sandwich bag

Dusting brush

Water brush

Dresden tool or
  cocktail stick

Scrunched up
  paper tissue

Clean pan scourer

Instructions:

1 For the wings, roll out the white modelling paste and cut with a large butterfly cutter. Gently brush blue powder food colour over the surface. Leave to dry for a few hours or overnight.

2 Make an egg shape of flesh-coloured sugarpaste for the body with a candy stick for support, slightly sticking out. Make a dip in the sugarpaste in the teacup, dampen it and attach the body, leaning against the inside of the teacup. Make sure the tops of the shoulders are above the rim of the cup.

3 Make the head as on page 8.

4 Roll out blue sugarpaste for the hat. Cut out two of the circles. Frill one circle and attach to the top of the head. Turn the edges of the other circle under to look gathered and attach to the top of the frilled circle.

5 Divide the rest of the flesh-coloured sugarpaste and form two carrot shapes for the arms. Bend to form the elbows and flatten the hands. Attach to the body.

6 Attach the wings as on page 9.

7 For the bubbles, make lots of pea-sized pieces of white sugarpaste, dust with edible pearl colour, top up the bath with the bubbles and sprinkle with edible glitter.

8 If you want to make a bath mat or towel, roll out blue sugarpaste, texture it with a clean scourer and mark a fringe on each end by pressing lines with a Dresden tool or cocktail stick.

Have fun looking for pretty teacups or bowls for this fairy to use for her bath. She would make a great gift for someone who likes a good soak.

Fairy Bride

Materials:

White modelling paste
(see page 4): 35g
(1¼oz) for the body
and 10g (⅓oz) for the
arms and skirt

5g (⅙oz) flesh-coloured
sugarpaste

5g (⅙oz) white
sugarpaste

5g (⅙oz) pink modelling
paste for the flowers

5g (⅙oz) green
modelling paste for
the flowers

Candy stick

Edible wafer paper or
rice paper

Edible powder food
colour, pearl white

Edible glitter

Egg white

Thick edible glue

Tools:

Garrett frill cutter (large
fluted round cutter)

Tiny blossom cutter

Scissors

Food colour felt-tip pen

Dusting brush

Non-stick rolling pin

Small drinking straw

Thin palette knife

Plastic sandwich bag

Water brush

Dresden tool

Cocktail stick

Instructions:

1 For the wings, trace the butterfly template
(right) on to edible wafer paper or rice paper
and cut out the shape. Carefully paint egg
white around the edge and sprinkle with edible
glitter. Shake off the excess. Leave to dry for a
few hours or overnight.

2 For the body, make a pear shape from white
modelling paste with a candy stick for support, slightly
sticking out for the neck.

3 Roll out white modelling paste thinly. Cut out
one garrett frill. Dust all over with edible pearl white
powder. Frill around the edge with a cocktail stick. Cut
a line straight from the edge to the middle. Dampen
the waist on the body. Attach the skirt, gathering the
waist along the cut edges as necessary.

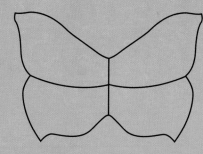

The template for the wings

32

4 Cut out a thin strip of rolled-out white modelling paste to make the ribbon for the waistband. Dust with pearl white powder. Dampen around the waist and attach the ribbon. Join at the back and cut off any excess.

5 Divide 5g (⅙oz) of white sugarpaste and form two carrot shapes for the arms. Bend to form the elbows and flatten the hands. Attach to the body. Attach a small pea-sized piece of pink sugarpaste to the fairy's hands for the bouquet.

6 Attach the wings, using egg white as glue.

7 Make the head as on page 8, but use the drinking straw to mark the closed eyes.

8 Use thick edible glue to stick the head on top of the neck.

9 For the hair, make long strands of white sugarpaste. Attach to the head, shaping into a style. Twirl some of the strands around a cocktail stick to make ringlets before attaching them.

10 Thinly roll out the pink and green sugarpaste. Cut out tiny green blossoms and attach them to the top of the head to form a head-dress, and over the base of the bouquet. Then cut out tiny pink blossoms and attach them over the green ones, hiding the green as much as possible.

This blushing bride would be perfect for a fairy lover's wedding cake.

Autumn Fairy

Materials:

10g (⅓oz) flesh-coloured sugarpaste

Brown sugarpaste or modelling chocolate:
10g (⅓oz) for the body,
10g (⅓oz) for the legs,
5g (⅙oz) for the arms and
5g (⅙oz) for the hat

10g (⅓oz) mixed red, yellow and orange sugarpaste (deliberately not mixed too thoroughly)

Candy stick

Tiny amount of black sugarpaste for the eyes

Tools:

Oak leaf cutters

Non-stick rolling pin

Small drinking straw

Thin palette knife

Plastic sandwich bag

Water brush

Dresden tool or cocktail stick

Instructions:

1 Make an egg shape of brown sugarpaste for the body with a candy stick for support, slightly sticking out. Lay the body on its side.

2 For the legs, divide the piece of brown sugarpaste. Roll each piece to a long carrot shape about twice the length of the body. Bend in the middle for the knees.

3 For the shoes, make two pea-sized pieces of the mixed sugarpaste and shape each one to a point. Dampen the ends of the legs and attach the shoes. Attach the legs to the body.

4 For the arms, divide the piece of brown sugarpaste and form two carrot shapes, slightly longer than the body. Bend to form the elbows, and flatten the hands. Attach to the body.

5 Roll out some of the mixed sugarpaste. Cut out at least seven oak leaves for the skirt, one for the sleeve and four for the wings. Attach to the body.

6 Make the head as on page 8.

7 For the hair, make lots of small carrot-shaped pieces of mixed sugarpaste. Dampen the head and attach the strands of hair with the pointed ends towards the face and neck. When the head is covered with enough strands of hair, dampen the end of the candy stick neck and attach the head.

8 Form a large acorn cup for the hat from a slightly larger than pea-sized piece of brown paste. Texture the surface with a cocktail stick. Make a small hole in the middle. Stick the acorn cup hat on the back of the head. Make a small stalk from brown sugarpaste and attach it to the middle of the acorn cup.

This impish little fairy looks as though it is curled up under a tree with the fallen leaves. The mixed sugarpaste colours are most effective if they are slightly unevenly mixed, for a natural look.

Fairy Godmother

Materials:

Pink modelling paste (see page 4): 35g (1¼oz) for the body, 10g (⅓oz) for the arms and cape

5g (⅙oz) flesh-coloured sugarpaste

5g (⅙oz) white sugarpaste

Candy stick

Edible powder food colour pearl white

Egg white

Tools:

Garrett frill cutter (large fluted round cutter)

Large butterfly cutter

Tiny star cutter

Scissors

Dusting brush

Non-stick rolling pin

Small drinking straw

Thin palette knife

Plastic sandwich bag

Water brush

Dresden tool or cocktail stick

Instructions:

1 For the wings, roll out the white modelling paste and cut out a large butterfly and a tiny star. Gently brush pearl white powder food colour over the surfaces. Frill over the edge of the butterfly using a Dresden tool or cocktail stick. Leave to dry for a few hours or overnight.

2 For the body, make a pear shape from pink modelling paste with a candy stick for support, slightly sticking out for the neck.

3 For the cape, roll out pink modelling paste thinly. Cut out one garrett frill. Dampen the back of the body. Wrap the cape around the body, slightly higher at the shoulders.

4 Divide 5g (⅙oz) of the pink modelling paste and form two carrot shapes for the arms. Bend to form the elbows, and flatten the hands. Attach to the body.

5 Attach the wings as on page 9, and the star on one hand.

6 Make the head as on page 8.

7 For the hair, make small carrots of white sugarpaste. Attach to the head, shaping into a style. Mark extra strands of hair with a Dresden tool or cocktail stick. Attach a pea-sized piece to form a bun on top.

8 Use thick edible glue to stick the head on top of the neck.

This beautiful fairy godmother looks as though she could fix anything for you! She would make a lovely gift for a godmother or just a friend who has helped you out.

Fairy Maid

Materials:

35g (1¼oz) black modelling paste for the body

5g (⅙oz) flesh-coloured sugarpaste

Black sugarpaste:
5g (⅙oz) for the arms and 5g (⅙oz) for the hair

5g (⅙oz) pale orange modelling paste

5g (⅙oz) white modelling paste for the wings, apron and butterfly

Candy stick

Edible powder food colour pearl white

Thick edible glue

Tools:

27mm (1in) heart cutter

Small butterfly cutter

22mm (⅞in) circle cutter

Dusting brush

Non-stick rolling pin

Small drinking straw

Thin palette knife

Plastic sandwich bag

Water brush

Dresden tool or cocktail stick

Instructions:

1 For the wings, roll out the white modelling paste and cut out two hearts with the heart cutter. Roll over the rounded edges with a cocktail stick to frill them slightly. Dust with edible pearl powder colour. Leave to dry for a few hours or overnight.

2 For the body, make a pear shape from black modelling paste with a candy stick for support, slightly sticking out for the neck.

3 For the apron, roll out white modelling paste thinly. Cut out a circle and a heart. Frill the edge of the circle and attach to the lower half of the body. Stick the heart over the circle, overlapping.

4 For the arms, divide 5g (⅙oz) of the black sugarpaste and form two carrot shapes. Bend to form the elbows, and flatten the hands. Attach to the body.

5 Roll out the pale orange paste for the duster. Cut to a small square, and stick it on to one hand.

6 Make the head as on page 8.

7 For the hair, shape the black sugarpaste between your fingers to cover the head. Cut to shape if too long. Mark lines with a Dresden tool or a cocktail stick to look like hair.

8 Attach the head to the body. Roll out white sugarpaste and cut out a small butterfly. Stick to the top of the head.

9 Attach the wings as on page 9.

This fairy looks kind and willing, and who wouldn't want some magical help around the house?

Cuddly Fairy

Materials:

Flesh-coloured sugarpaste:
   10g (⅓oz) for the head,
   20g (⅔oz) for the body,
   20g (⅔oz) for the legs
   and 10g (⅓oz) for
   the arms

10g (⅓oz) pink sugarpaste
   for the dress

5g (⅙oz) dark pink
   sugarpaste for the shoes

5g (⅙oz) white sugarpaste
   for the petticoat and
   head-dress

5g (⅙oz) brown sugarpaste
   or modelling chocolate
   for the hair

Candy stick

Tiny amount of black
   sugarpaste for the eyes

Edible wafer paper or
   rice paper

Egg white

Edible glitter

Tools:

27mm (1in) heart cutter

Circle cutters: 56mm
   (2¼in), 41mm (1⅝in)

Small blossom cutter

Scissors

Food colour felt-tip pen

Non-stick rolling pin

Small drinking straw

Thin palette knife

Plastic sandwich bag

Water brush

Dresden tool or
   cocktail stick

Instructions:

1 For the wings, trace the butterfly wings from page 32 on to edible wafer paper or rice paper and cut them out. Carefully paint egg white around the edge and sprinkle with edible glitter. Shake off the excess. Leave to dry for a few hours.

2 For the body, make an upside-down pear shape of flesh-coloured sugarpaste with a candy stick for support, slightly sticking out.

3 Divide the piece of paste for the legs. Roll each piece to a long carrot shape, about twice the length of the body. Attach small cones in dark pink sugarpaste for the shoes. Stick the legs together.

4 Roll out white sugarpaste thinly. Cut out at least two of the smaller circles. Frill around the edge with a cocktail stick. Dampen the middle of each and attach over the top of the legs. Repeat, using the pink sugarpaste and the larger circles. Dampen the bottom of the body and attach to middle of the skirt.

5 Attach a pink sugarpaste heart for the front of the dress, and small blossoms around the waist.

6 For the arms, divide the piece of flesh-coloured sugarpaste and form two carrot shapes, slightly longer than the body. Bend to form the elbows, and flatten the hands. Attach to the body.

7 Make the head as on page 8.

8 For the hair, make lots of small carrot-shaped pieces of brown sugarpaste. Dampen the head and attach the strands of hair with the pointed ends towards the face and neck. When the head is covered, attach a circlet of white blossoms for the head-dress.

9 Dampen the end of the candy stick neck, and attach the head.

10 Attach the wings using egg white as glue.

Just to prove that fairies are not all tiny and ethereal, here's a big, buxom and beautiful fairy who is sweetness itself.

Sunshine Fairy

Materials:

10g (⅓oz) flesh-coloured
  sugarpaste

Yellow sugarpaste:
  10g (⅓oz) for the body,
  10g (⅓oz) for the legs,
  5g (⅙oz) for the arms and
  10g (⅓oz) for the skirt,
  hat and wings

Candy stick

Small amount of black
  sugarpaste

Tools:

Large eight-petal
  flower cutter

Food colour felt-tip pen

Non-stick rolling pin

Small drinking straw

Thin palette knife

Plastic sandwich bag

Water brush

Dresden tool or
  cocktail stick

Instructions:

1 Make an egg shape of yellow
sugarpaste for the body with a candy
stick for support, slightly sticking out.
Lay the body on its back.

2 For the legs, divide the piece of paste
in two. Roll each piece to a long carrot
shape about twice the length of the
body. Bend in the middle for the knee,
and bend to form the foot. Attach the
legs to the body, with knees up and feet on the surface.

3 For the wings, roll out yellow sugarpaste and cut out one large flower.
Cut it in half and attach under the body.

4 Cut out at least four large flowers, cut them in quarters and attach to the
body to form the skirt.

5 For the arms, divide the piece of sugarpaste and form two carrot shapes,
slightly longer than the body. Bend to form the elbows, and flatten the
hands. Attach to the body.

6 Make the head as on page 8. Instead of making eyes, make two larger circles of black, cut the top edge off, stick on and draw the frames for the sunglasses with the food-colour felt-tip pen.

7 For the hair, cut out two more large yellow flowers and stick one over the head, and the second one lying flat under the head. Dampen the end of the candy stick neck and attach the head.

This brilliant fairy just loves to stretch out and catch some rays. You could make her for a sun worshipper you know.

Tooth Fairy

Materials:

10g (⅓oz) flesh-coloured
 sugarpaste

Purple sugarpaste: 10g (⅓oz)
 for the body and 10g (⅓oz)
 for the shoes and arms

10g (⅓oz) white sugarpaste

Six candy sticks

Tiny amount of black
 sugarpaste for the eyes

Leaf gelatine for the wings

Edible glitter

Egg white

Tools:

18mm (¾in) heart cutter

Small star cutter

Scissors

Non-stick rolling pin

Small drinking straw

Thin palette knife

Plastic sandwich bag

Water brush

Dresden tool or
 cocktail stick

Scrunched up paper tissue

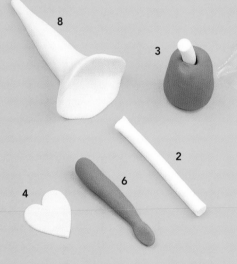

Instructions:

1 For the wings, cut the leaf gelatine with scissors to a simple butterfly shape. Carefully paint the edge with egg white and sprinkle with edible glitter. Shake off the excess and leave to dry for a few hours.

2 Make the legs from two candy sticks. For the shoes, make two pea-sized pieces of purple sugarpaste and shape each one to a point. Attach the shoes.

3 For the body, make an egg shape of purple sugarpaste with a candy stick for support, slightly sticking out. Push the top ends of the legs into the body.

4 Roll out white sugarpaste. Cut out at least seven heart shapes, and attach on to the body for the skirt.

5 Make a sugar toothbrush using a candy stick. Shape a slightly larger than pea-sized piece of white sugarpaste to a solid block shape. Attach to the end of the sugar stick, and mark bristles using a knife.

6 Divide the piece of paste for the arms and form two carrot shapes, slightly longer than the body. Bend to form the elbows, and flatten the hands. Attach to the body, and stick one hand to the toothbrush.

7 Make the head as on page 8.

8 For the hat, use white sugarpaste the same size as the head. Shape to a long cone. Flatten the wide end between your finger and thumb until it is big enough to cover the back of the head. Shape the pointed end to a spiral, to look like toothpaste. Attach the head to the top of the body.

9 Roll out white sugarpaste and cut out lots of small stars, one for each shoe and the rest all around the edge between the hat and the head, overlapping.

10 Attach the wings as on page 9.

Have you ever wondered who was leaving coins under your pillow? Well here she is, a fairy with a sweet tooth but also a toothbrush to keep teeth sparkling white and clean!

Fairy Cake Fairy

Materials:

10g (⅓oz) flesh-coloured sugarpaste

White sugarpaste:
10g (⅓oz) for the body,
5g (⅙oz) for the shoes and hands

5g (⅙oz) pink modelling paste (see page 4) for the wings

Five candy sticks

Tiny amount of black sugarpaste for the eyes

Silver paper sweet case

Edible glitter

For the royal icing:
225g (8oz) icing/confectioners' sugar,
1 egg white, half teaspoon glycerine

Tools:

Grease-free bowl

27mm (1in) heart cutter

Non-stick rolling pin

Small drinking straw

Thin palette knife

Plastic sandwich bag

Water brush

Dresden tool or cocktail stick

Piping bag and small star piping tube

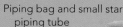

Instructions:

1 To make the royal icing, beat the egg white in a grease-free bowl, add the icing sugar a little at a time and beat for a few minutes until it becomes a thick, creamy consistency and forms peaks. Mix in the glycerine.

2 For the wings, roll out pink modelling paste and cut out two hearts. Leave to dry for a few hours or overnight.

3 Make the legs from two candy sticks. For the shoes, make two pea-sized pieces of white sugarpaste and shape each to a point. Attach the shoes.

4 Cut two holes on the bottom edge of the paper sweet case for the legs to be pushed in. Fill the case with a ball of sugarpaste and push the legs in through the holes into the paste. Push in another candy stick vertically as support for the neck.

5 For the arms, cut candy sticks to 32mm (1¼in). Make two pea-sized pieces of white sugarpaste and form each into a simple hand shape. Cut out tiny triangles to form thumbs. Attach to the arms.

6 Make the head as on page 8.

7 Fill a piping bag with royal icing. Using a star piping tube, pipe a large swirl into the paper sweet case, up to the fairy's neck. Push the arms into the swirl and attach the wings while the icing is still soft. For best results, allow this part to dry for a few hours before attaching the head.

8 Attach the head with a little royal icing. For the hair, pipe a few strands towards the face, then pipe a spiral swirl to cover the head. Sprinkle with edible glitter while the icing is still soft.

Chocolate Sweetheart
Did you know that the design for fairy cakes came from an actual fairy?! The alternative has chocolate biscuit legs and arms, and cream-coloured icing. She could also be made by baking little cupcakes in the foil sweet cases. The icing swirls could be made with buttercream instead of royal icing.

Acknowledgements
Many thanks to Anne Killick for all her help, and
to Roz, Sophie and Marrianne at Search Press.

Publisher's Note
If you would like more information about
sugarcraft, try *Sugar Animals*, Search Press, 2009
or *Decorated Cup Cakes*, Search Press, 2009,
both by Frances McNaughton.